D1556393

A LITTLE BOOK OF

Scottish
Sayings

Compiled by
J. D. Sutherland

Appletree Press

First published in 1998 by
The Appletree Press Ltd
19–21 Alfred Street, Belfast BT2 8DL
Tel: +44 (0) 1232 243074
Fax: +44 (0) 1232 246756
e-mail: frontdesk@appletree.ie
web site: www.irelandseye.com

Copyright © 1998 The Appletree Press Ltd

A Little Book of Scottish Sayings

A catalogue record for this book is available
from The British Library

ISBN 0-86281-699-8

9 8 7 6 5 4 3 2 1

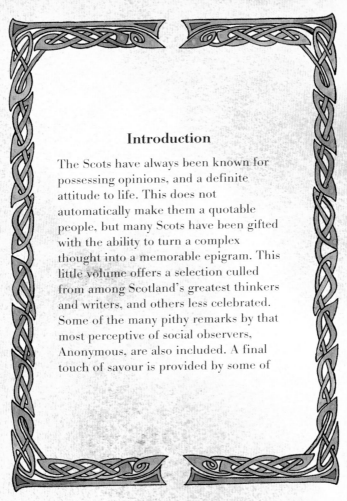

Introduction

The Scots have always been known for possessing opinions, and a definite attitude to life. This does not automatically make them a quotable people, but many Scots have been gifted with the ability to turn a complex thought into a memorable epigram. This little volume offers a selection culled from among Scotland's greatest thinkers and writers, and others less celebrated. Some of the many pithy remarks by that most perceptive of social observers, Anonymous, are also included. A final touch of savour is provided by some of

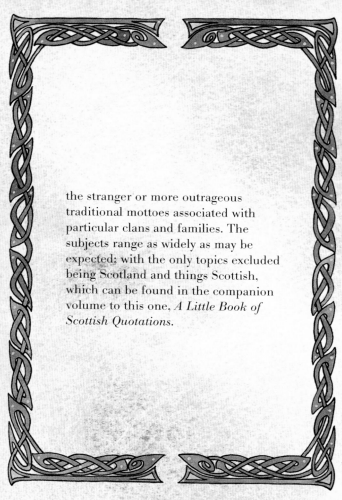

the stranger or more outrageous
traditional mottoes associated with
particular clans and families. The
subjects range as widely as may be
expected; with the only topics excluded
being Scotland and things Scottish,
which can be found in the companion
volume to this one, *A Little Book of
Scottish Quotations*.

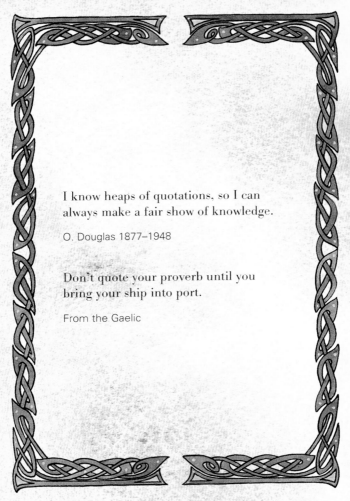

I know heaps of quotations, so I can always make a fair show of knowledge.

O. Douglas 1877–1948

Don't quote your proverb until you bring your ship into port.

From the Gaelic

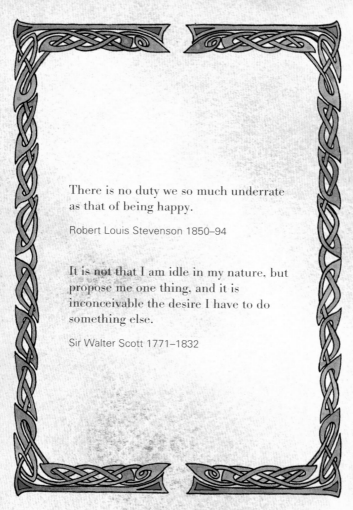

There is no duty we so much underrate
as that of being happy.

Robert Louis Stevenson 1850–94

It is not that I am idle in my nature, but
propose me one thing, and it is
inconceivable the desire I have to do
something else.

Sir Walter Scott 1771–1832

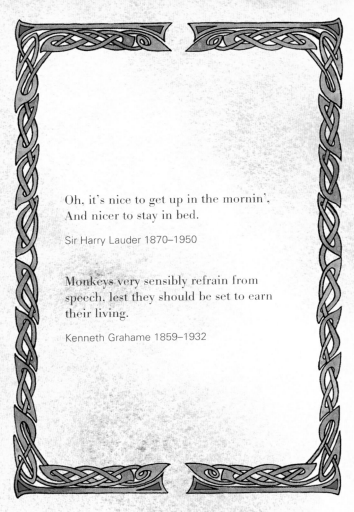

Oh, it's nice to get up in the mornin',
And nicer to stay in bed.

Sir Harry Lauder 1870–1950

Monkeys very sensibly refrain from
speech, lest they should be set to earn
their living.

Kenneth Grahame 1859–1932

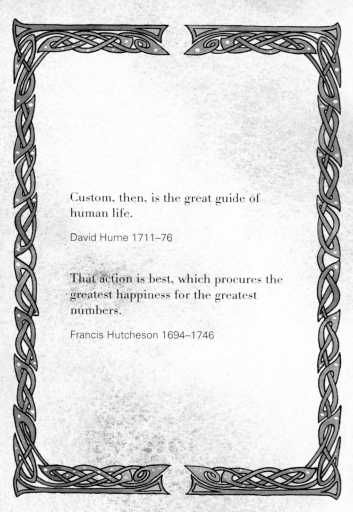

Custom, then, is the great guide of human life.

David Hume 1711–76

That action is best, which procures the greatest happiness for the greatest numbers.

Francis Hutcheson 1694–1746

Happy the people whose annals are
blank in the history books.

Thomas Carlyle 1795–1881

O grant me, Heaven, a middle state,
Neither too humble, or too great;
More than enough for nature's ends,
With something left to treat my friends.

David Mallet 1705–65

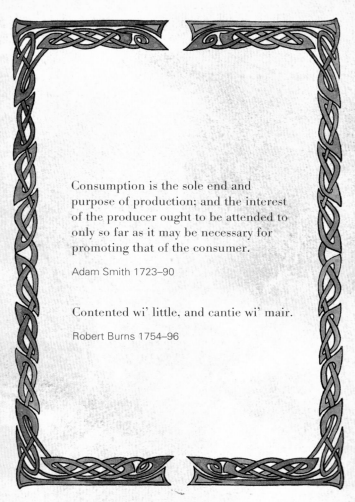

Consumption is the sole end and purpose of production; and the interest of the producer ought to be attended to only so far as it may be necessary for promoting that of the consumer.

Adam Smith 1723–90

Contented wi' little, and cantie wi' mair.

Robert Burns 1754–96

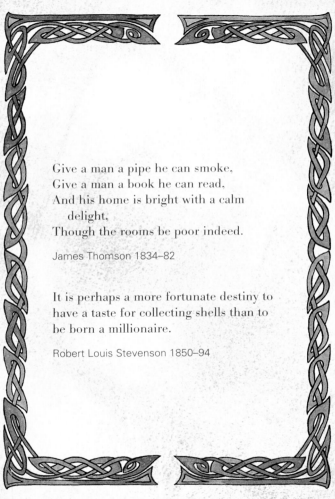

Give a man a pipe he can smoke,
Give a man a book he can read,
And his home is bright with a calm
    delight,
Though the rooms be poor indeed.

James Thomson 1834–82

It is perhaps a more fortunate destiny to
have a taste for collecting shells than to
be born a millionaire.

Robert Louis Stevenson 1850–94

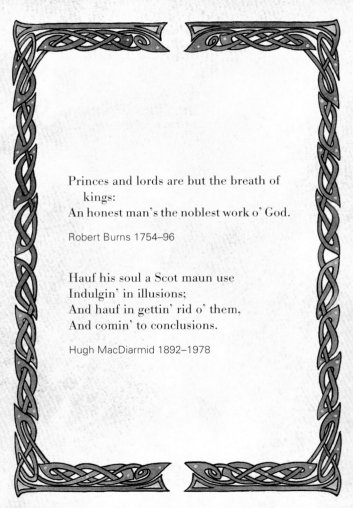

Princes and lords are but the breath of
    kings:
An honest man's the noblest work o' God.

Robert Burns 1754–96

Hauf his soul a Scot maun use
Indulgin' in illusions;
And hauf in gettin' rid o' them,
And comin' to conclusions.

Hugh MacDiarmid 1892–1978

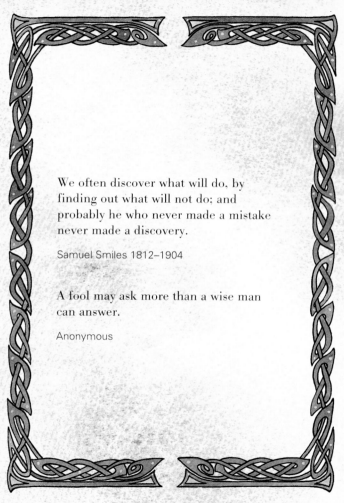

We often discover what will do, by finding out what will not do; and probably he who never made a mistake never made a discovery.

Samuel Smiles 1812–1904

A fool may ask more than a wise man can answer.

Anonymous

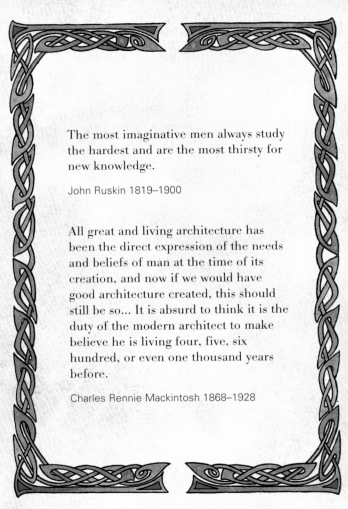

The most imaginative men always study
the hardest and are the most thirsty for
new knowledge.

John Ruskin 1819–1900

All great and living architecture has
been the direct expression of the needs
and beliefs of man at the time of its
creation, and now if we would have
good architecture created, this should
still be so... It is absurd to think it is the
duty of the modern architect to make
believe he is living four, five, six
hundred, or even one thousand years
before.

Charles Rennie Mackintosh 1868–1928

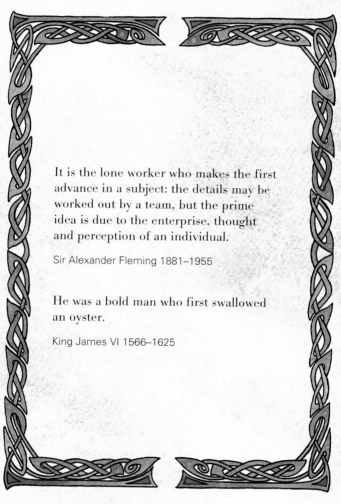

It is the lone worker who makes the first advance in a subject: the details may be worked out by a team, but the prime idea is due to the enterprise, thought and perception of an individual.

Sir Alexander Fleming 1881–1955

He was a bold man who first swallowed an oyster.

King James VI 1566–1625

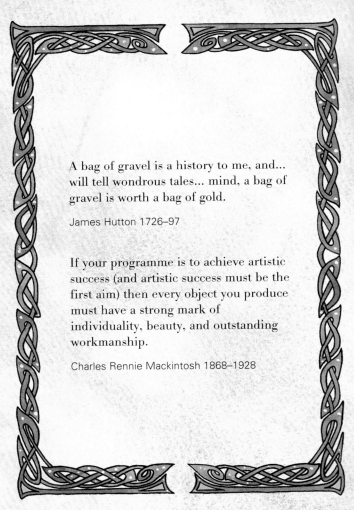

A bag of gravel is a history to me, and...
will tell wondrous tales... mind, a bag of
gravel is worth a bag of gold.

James Hutton 1726–97

If your programme is to achieve artistic
success (and artistic success must be the
first aim) then every object you produce
must have a strong mark of
individuality, beauty, and outstanding
workmanship.

Charles Rennie Mackintosh 1868–1928

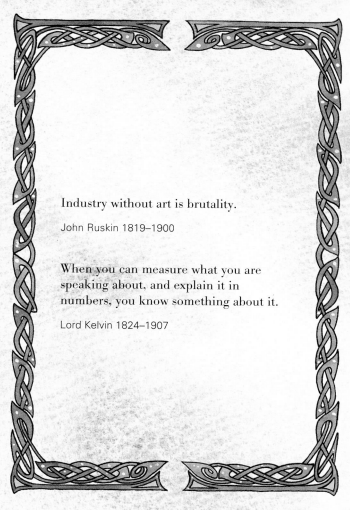

Industry without art is brutality.

John Ruskin 1819–1900

When you can measure what you are speaking about, and explain it in numbers, you know something about it.

Lord Kelvin 1824–1907

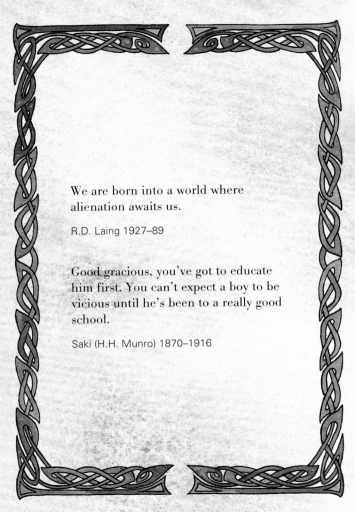

We are born into a world where
alienation awaits us.

R.D. Laing 1927–89

Good gracious, you've got to educate
him first. You can't expect a boy to be
vicious until he's been to a really good
school.

Saki (H.H. Munro) 1870–1916

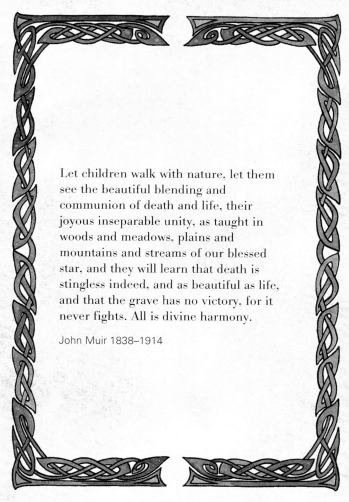

Let children walk with nature, let them see the beautiful blending and communion of death and life, their joyous inseparable unity, as taught in woods and meadows, plains and mountains and streams of our blessed star, and they will learn that death is stingless indeed, and as beautiful as life, and that the grave has no victory, for it never fights. All is divine harmony.

John Muir 1838–1914

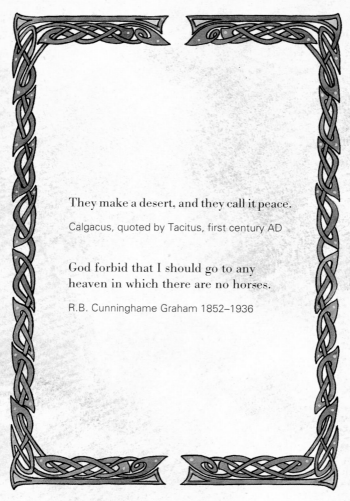

They make a desert, and they call it peace.

Calgacus, quoted by Tacitus, first century AD

God forbid that I should go to any
heaven in which there are no horses.

R.B. Cunninghame Graham 1852–1936

A LITTLE BOOK OF

Scottish
Sayings

Appletree Press

To live in hearts we leave behind
Is not to die.

Thomas Campbell 1777–1844

A man with God is always in the majority.

John Knox *c.* 1513–72

The principal part of faith is patience.

George Macdonald 1824–1905

This little life is all we must endure,
The grave's most holy peace is ever sure,
We fall asleep and never wake again.

James Thomson 1834–82

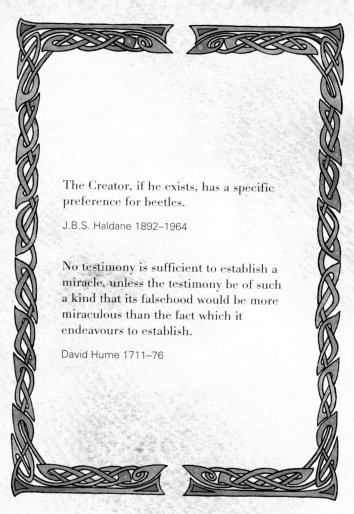

The Creator, if he exists, has a specific preference for beetles.

J.B.S. Haldane 1892–1964

No testimony is sufficient to establish a miracle, unless the testimony be of such a kind that its falsehood would be more miraculous than the fact which it endeavours to establish.

David Hume 1711–76

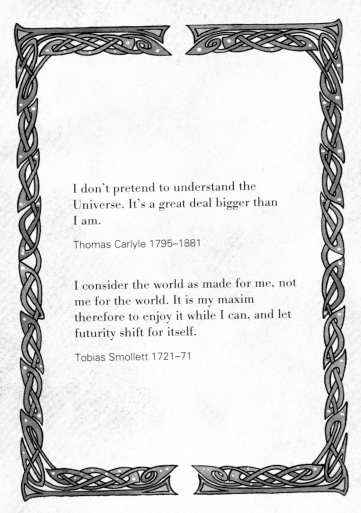

I don't pretend to understand the
Universe. It's a great deal bigger than
I am.

Thomas Carlyle 1795–1881

I consider the world as made for me, not
me for the world. It is my maxim
therefore to enjoy it while I can, and let
futurity shift for itself.

Tobias Smollett 1721–71

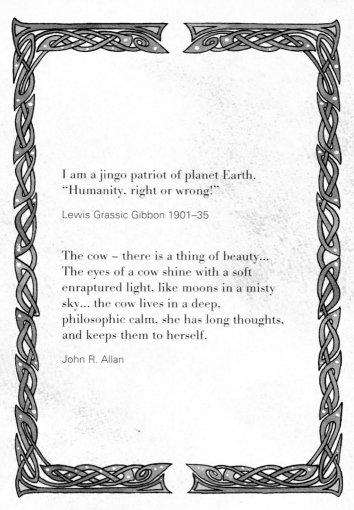

I am a jingo patriot of planet Earth.
"Humanity, right or wrong!"

Lewis Grassic Gibbon 1901–35

The cow – there is a thing of beauty...
The eyes of a cow shine with a soft
enraptured light, like moons in a misty
sky... the cow lives in a deep,
philosophic calm, she has long thoughts,
and keeps them to herself.

John R. Allan

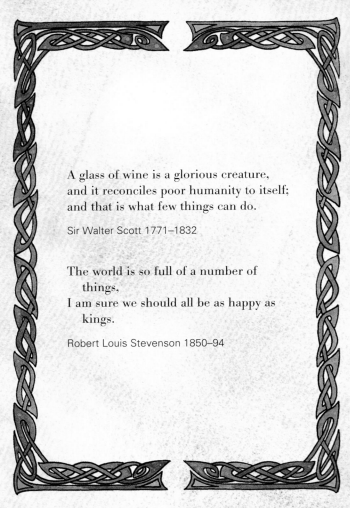

A glass of wine is a glorious creature,
and it reconciles poor humanity to itself;
and that is what few things can do.

Sir Walter Scott 1771–1832

The world is so full of a number of
    things,
I am sure we should all be as happy as
    kings.

Robert Louis Stevenson 1850–94

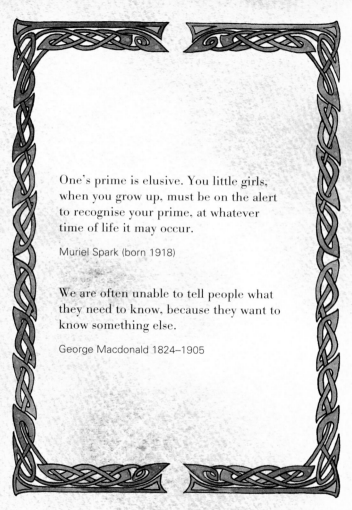

One's prime is elusive. You little girls, when you grow up, must be on the alert to recognise your prime, at whatever time of life it may occur.

Muriel Spark (born 1918)

We are often unable to tell people what they need to know, because they want to know something else.

George Macdonald 1824–1905

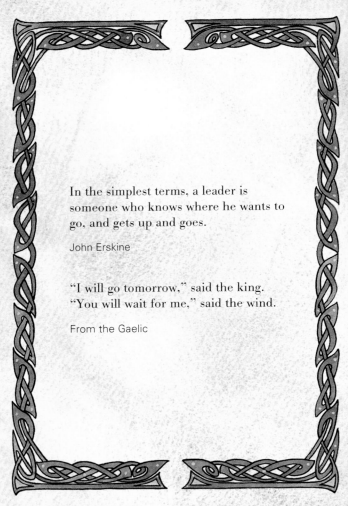

In the simplest terms, a leader is someone who knows where he wants to go, and gets up and goes.

John Erskine

"I will go tomorrow," said the king.
"You will wait for me," said the wind.

From the Gaelic

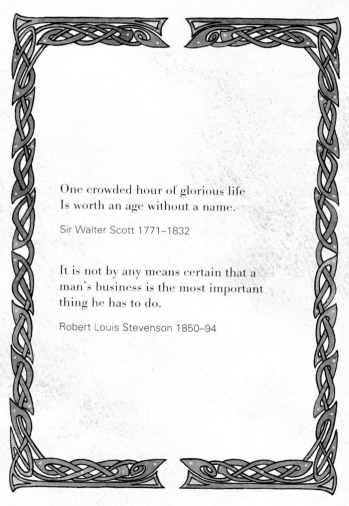

One crowded hour of glorious life
Is worth an age without a name.

Sir Walter Scott 1771–1832

It is not by any means certain that a
man's business is the most important
thing he has to do.

Robert Louis Stevenson 1850–94

It's no fish ye're buying; it's men's lives.

Sir Walter Scott 1771–1832

The waves have some mercy, but the
rocks have no mercy at all.

From the Gaelic

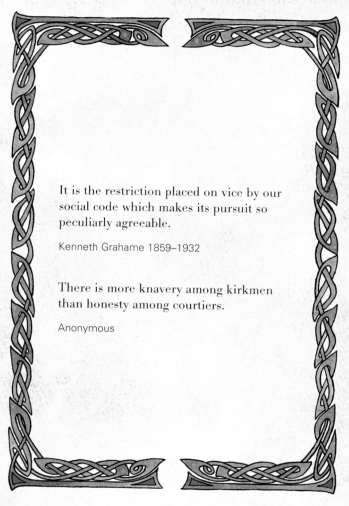

It is the restriction placed on vice by our social code which makes its pursuit so peculiarly agreeable.

Kenneth Grahame 1859–1932

There is more knavery among kirkmen than honesty among courtiers.

Anonymous

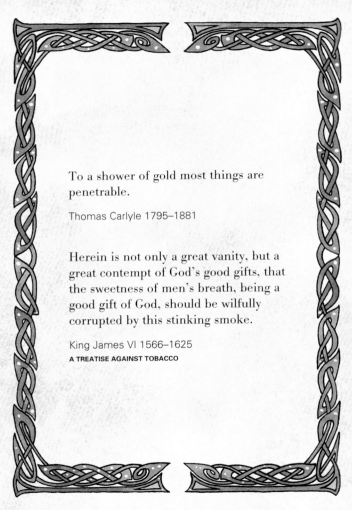

To a shower of gold most things are
penetrable.

Thomas Carlyle 1795–1881

Herein is not only a great vanity, but a
great contempt of God's good gifts, that
the sweetness of men's breath, being a
good gift of God, should be wilfully
corrupted by this stinking smoke.

King James VI 1566–1625
A TREATISE AGAINST TOBACCO

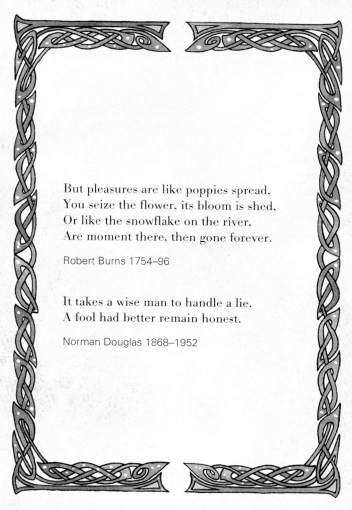

But pleasures are like poppies spread,
You seize the flower, its bloom is shed,
Or like the snowflake on the river,
Are moment there, then gone forever.

Robert Burns 1754–96

It takes a wise man to handle a lie.
A fool had better remain honest.

Norman Douglas 1868–1952

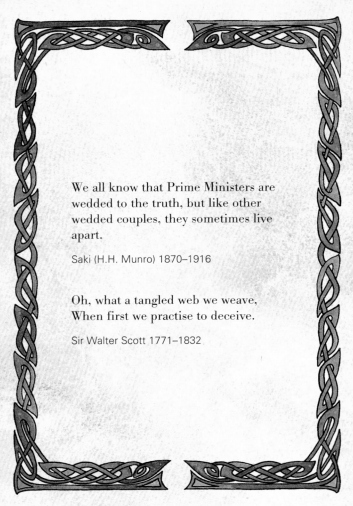

We all know that Prime Ministers are wedded to the truth, but like other wedded couples, they sometimes live apart.

Saki (H.H. Munro) 1870–1916

Oh, what a tangled web we weave,
When first we practise to deceive.

Sir Walter Scott 1771–1832

But Lord, remember me and mine
Wi' mercies temporal and divine,
That I for grace and gear may shine
Excelled by none;
And all the glory shall be thine,
Amen, Amen!

Robert Burns 1754–96

He either fears his fate too much,
Or his deserts are small,
That puts it not unto the touch,
To win, or lose, it all.

Marquis of Montrose 1612–50

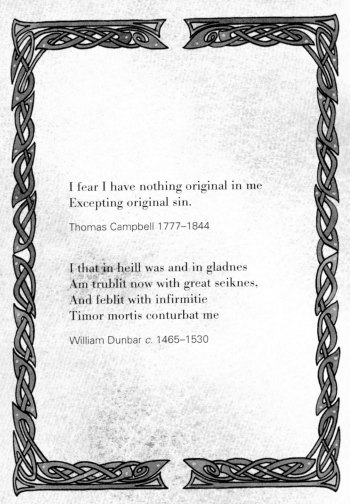

I fear I have nothing original in me
Excepting original sin.

Thomas Campbell 1777–1844

I that in heill was and in gladnes
Am trublit now with great seiknes,
And feblit with infirmitie
Timor mortis conturbat me

William Dunbar *c.* 1465–1530

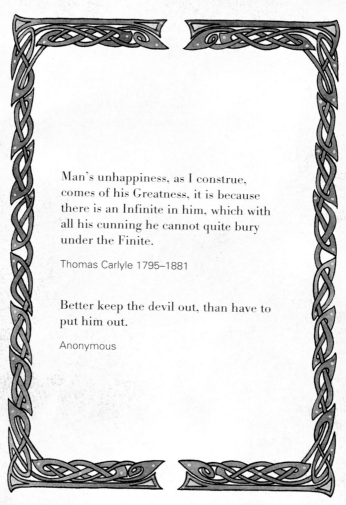

Man's unhappiness, as I construe,
comes of his Greatness, it is because
there is an Infinite in him, which with
all his cunning he cannot quite bury
under the Finite.

Thomas Carlyle 1795–1881

Better keep the devil out, than have to
put him out.

Anonymous

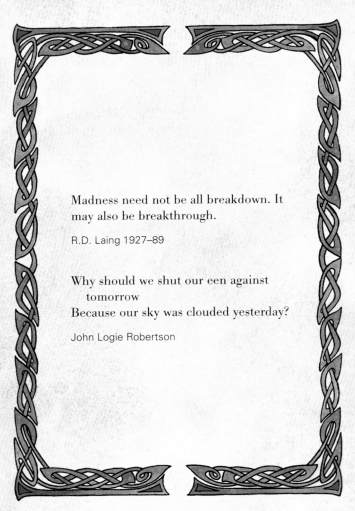

Madness need not be all breakdown. It may also be breakthrough.

R.D. Laing 1927–89

Why should we shut our een against
    tomorrow
Because our sky was clouded yesterday?

John Logie Robertson

Hearts of gold and hearts of lead
Sing it yet in sun and rain,
"Heel and toe from dawn to dusk,
Round the world and home again."

John Davidson 1857–1909

My heart is a lonely hunter, that hunts
on a lonely hill.

Fiona MacLeod 1856–1905

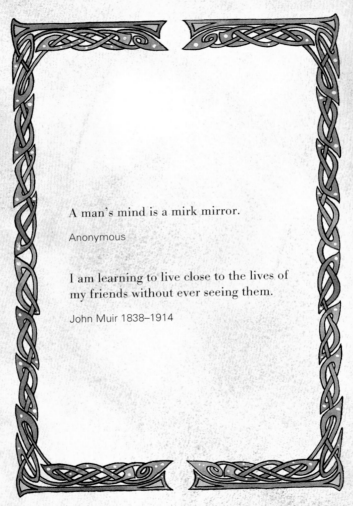

A man's mind is a mirk mirror.

Anonymous

I am learning to live close to the lives of
my friends without ever seeing them.

John Muir 1838–1914

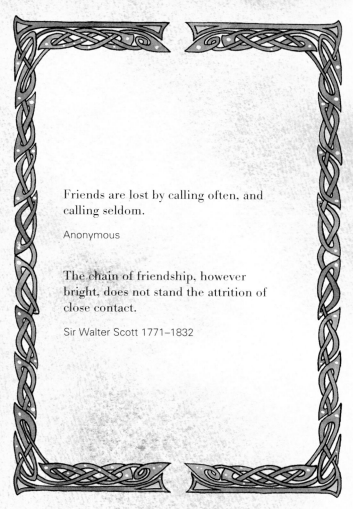

Friends are lost by calling often, and calling seldom.

Anonymous

The chain of friendship, however bright, does not stand the attrition of close contact.

Sir Walter Scott 1771–1832

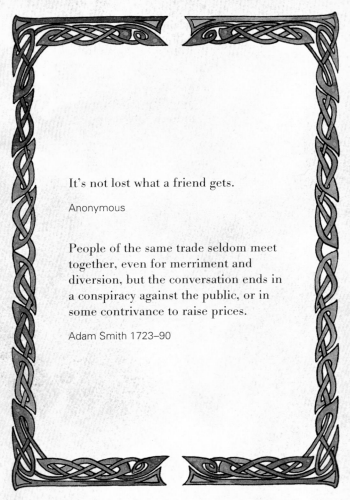

It's not lost what a friend gets.

Anonymous

People of the same trade seldom meet
together, even for merriment and
diversion, but the conversation ends in
a conspiracy against the public, or in
some contrivance to raise prices.

Adam Smith 1723–90

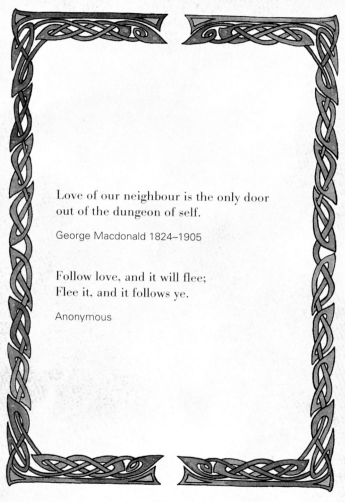

Love of our neighbour is the only door
out of the dungeon of self.

George Macdonald 1824–1905

Follow love, and it will flee;
Flee it, and it follows ye.

Anonymous

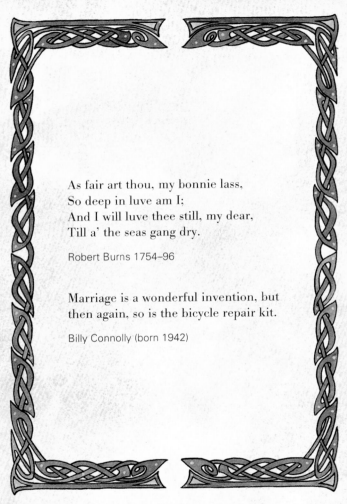

As fair art thou, my bonnie lass,
So deep in luve am I;
And I will luve thee still, my dear,
Till a' the seas gang dry.

Robert Burns 1754–96

Marriage is a wonderful invention, but
then again, so is the bicycle repair kit.

Billy Connolly (born 1942)

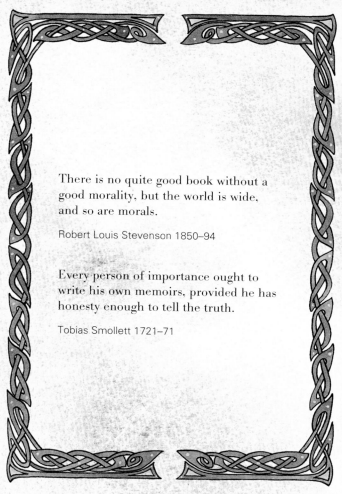

There is no quite good book without a
good morality, but the world is wide,
and so are morals.

Robert Louis Stevenson 1850–94

Every person of importance ought to
write his own memoirs, provided he has
honesty enough to tell the truth.

Tobias Smollett 1721–71

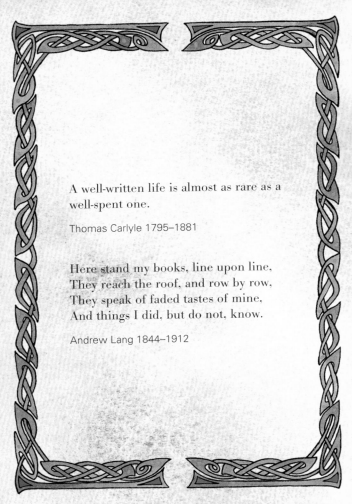

A well-written life is almost as rare as a well-spent one.

Thomas Carlyle 1795–1881

Here stand my books, line upon line,
They reach the roof, and row by row,
They speak of faded tastes of mine,
And things I did, but do not, know.

Andrew Lang 1844–1912

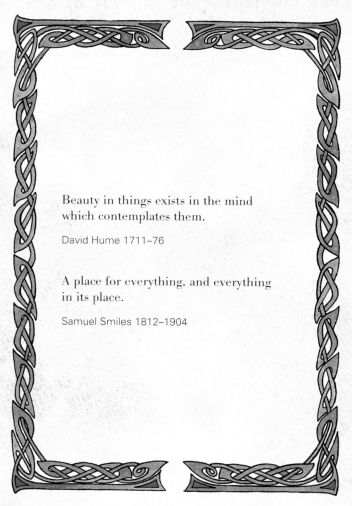

Beauty in things exists in the mind
which contemplates them.

David Hume 1711–76

A place for everything, and everything
in its place.

Samuel Smiles 1812–1904

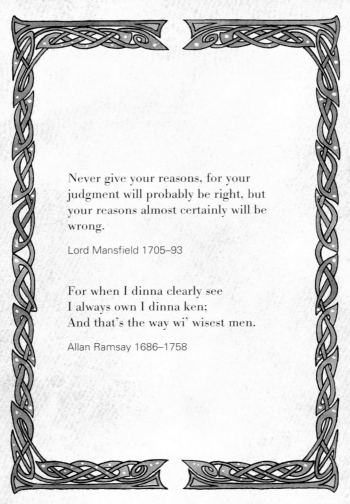

Never give your reasons, for your judgment will probably be right, but your reasons almost certainly will be wrong.

Lord Mansfield 1705–93

For when I dinna clearly see
I always own I dinna ken;
And that's the way wi' wisest men.

Allan Ramsay 1686–1758

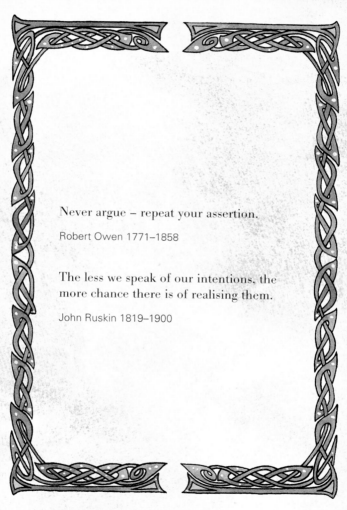

Never argue – repeat your assertion.

Robert Owen 1771–1858

The less we speak of our intentions, the more chance there is of realising them.

John Ruskin 1819–1900

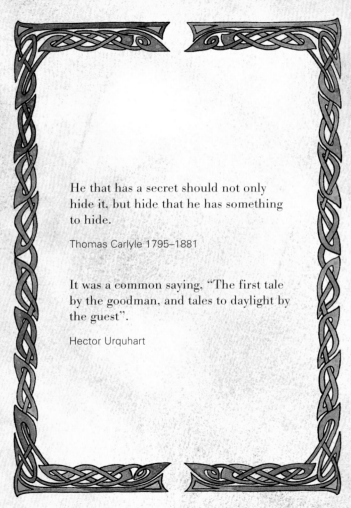

He that has a secret should not only hide it, but hide that he has something to hide.

Thomas Carlyle 1795–1881

It was a common saying, "The first tale by the goodman, and tales to daylight by the guest".

Hector Urquhart

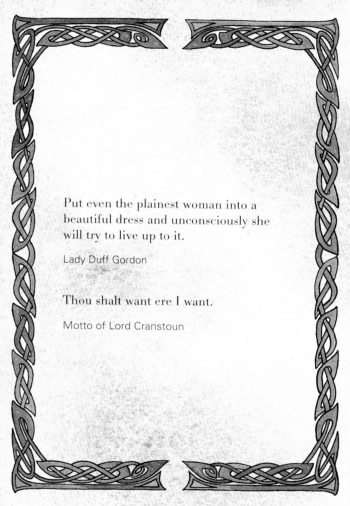

Put even the plainest woman into a beautiful dress and unconsciously she will try to live up to it.

Lady Duff Gordon

Thou shalt want ere I want.

Motto of Lord Cranstoun

Touch not the cat bot a glove.

Motto of Clan Macpherson

Furth fortune and fill the fetters.

Motto of Murray of Atholl

Grip Fast.

Motto of the Leslies

E'en do, and spare nought.

Motto of Clan MacGregor

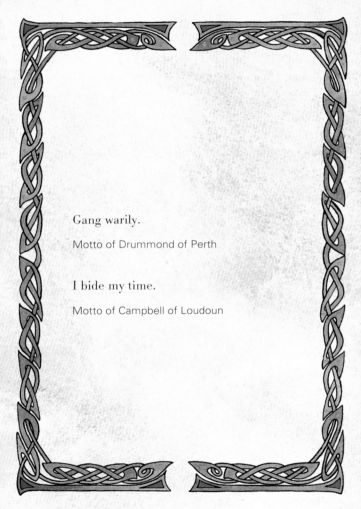

Gang warily.

Motto of Drummond of Perth

I bide my time.

Motto of Campbell of Loudoun

They say. What say they? Let them say.

Motto of Keith, Earl Marischal

Come hither, come hither,
You shall get flesh, you shall get flesh.
Come sons of dogs, you shall get flesh.
You shall get flesh.

War cry of Clan Cameron (from the Gaelic)

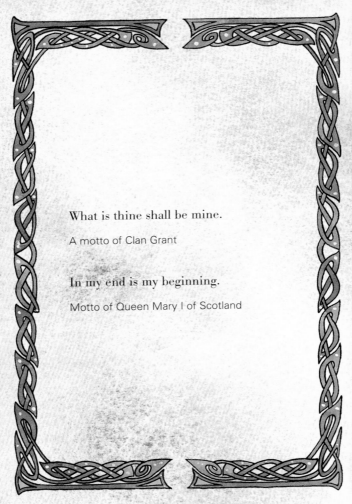

What is thine shall be mine.

A motto of Clan Grant

In my end is my beginning.

Motto of Queen Mary I of Scotland